Learn HTML, CSS, and JavaScript With This One Book

Please note; that this book is just the JavaScript chapter of the full book; the **Basics of Front-End Web Development (HTML, CSS, and JavasScript)**. To learn all three coding languages, checkout the full book.

https://www.amazon.com/Basics-Front-End-Development-HTML-JavaScript-ebook/dp/B0DJ147B15

Learn SEO Too

Learning front-end web development is only half the battle to producing an amazing web experience. Also, you need to learn **SEO (search engine optimization)**.

Learning SEO ensures that visitors can actually find your website and apps on the internet. Below I included links to several SEO books I've written. They are excellent reads.

The ABCs of SEO: Search Engine Optimization 101

https://www.amazon.com/ABCs-Search-Engine-Optimization-Page-ebook/dp/B0C2JSLW7M

The Technical SEO Handbook

https://www.amazon.com/Technical-SEO-Handbook-Learn-Issues-ebook/dp/B0CMBJR9QV

The SEO and Web Developer Collaboration Guide

https://www.amazon.com/SEO-Web-Developer-Collaboration-Guide-ebook/dp/B0DHLBM48C

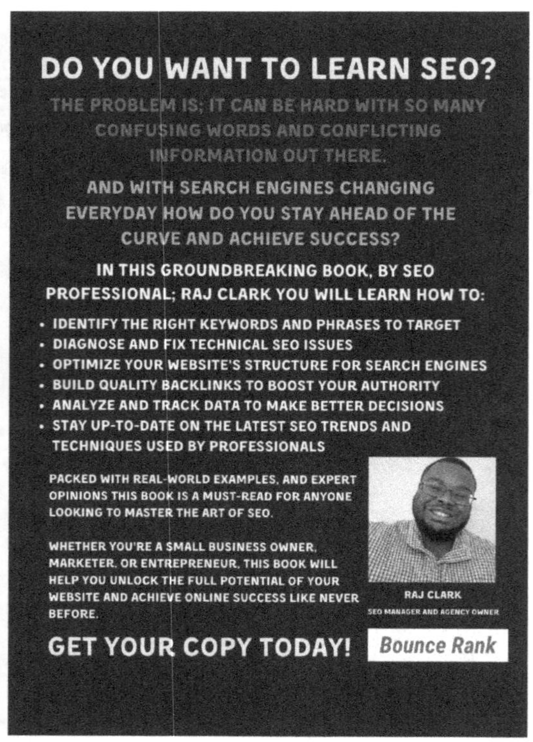

The Basics of JavaScript Coding For Beginners

By: Roggie Clark

Copyright

Title: The Basics of JavaScript Coding For Beginners
Author: Roggie Clark

Cover Design: Roggie Clark
Editing: Renee' Clark

Printed in the United States of America

Disclaimer

The views and opinions expressed in this book are those of the author and do not necessarily reflect the official policy or position of any individual, company, or organization cited or referenced in the text.

The author is not affiliated with any of the individuals, companies, or organizations mentioned in the text, nor does the author receive any form of compensation for citing or referencing them. Some sample scenarios in this text are fictitious. Any similarity to actual persons, living or dead, is coincidental.

The professional information (strategies, tips, and concepts) in this text is distributed on an "as is" basis, without warranty. While every precaution has been taken in the preparation of the text to ensure all information is accurate, neither the author nor the publisher shall have any liability to any person or entity with respect to any loss or damage caused or alleged to be caused directly or indirectly by the instructions contained in this text or by the computer software and hardware products described in it.

Neither the author nor the publisher guarantees any specific results or outcomes, and the information provided in this text should not be construed as professional advice. Readers should always consult with a qualified professional before making any significant changes to their website or business.

By reading this text, you agree that the author nor the publisher is responsible for any direct, indirect, incidental, or consequential damages that may arise from the use of the information provided. You assume full responsibility for any actions taken based on the information presented in this text.

Table of Contents

Chapter 1: Introduction

Is you're website suffering from a boring, static experience? This is not 1999, in this modern web age having an exciting, and engaging web experience is a must! Learning JavaScript is your key to unlocking interactivity, dynamism, and functionality in your website.

With JavaScript, you're not simply creating static webpages—you're building the backbone of user experiences that are smooth, responsive, and engaging.

Whether it's creating interactive forms, adding animations, or building entire web applications, this language is the driving force behind modern, dynamic websites. The exciting part? You have total control. JavaScript allows you to manipulate the behavior of a webpage in real-time. You can use JavaScript to "listen" for "events" to capture user input, respond to clicks, update content without refreshing the page, and so much more.

Once you master the basics of JavaScript, you'll be able to:

- Implement essential features like modals, sliders, and even games, adding a whole new dimension to the user experience.

- Seamlessly integrate your JavaScript skills with HTML and CSS, ensuring a fluid, dynamic front-end that works smoothly on every device.

- Have the prowess to dive into advanced JavaScript frameworks and libraries that power some of the most popular websites and apps today.

The best part about learning JavaScript is that it is incredibly versatile and approachable, whether you're new to coding or transitioning from a design-focused background. Its logic will click with you faster than you might think, and before long, you'll be crafting websites that are not just functional but truly interactive.

So get ready to transform how you think about web development. By the end of this book, you won't just be building websites—you'll be crafting dynamic, exciting web experiences that stand out in the ever-evolving digital world.

The power of JavaScript is at your fingertips, and the possibilities are endless! Let's get started with Chapter 2 which is the basics of JavaScript and why it was created.

Chapter 2: JavaScript Basics

JavaScript is a versatile, high-level programming language developed by Brendan Eich, in 1995 as a way to make static HTML web pages more interactive. It is not to be confused with *Java,* despite similar names, they vary greatly in their purpose and usage.

JavaScript is used to create interactive, and dynamic effects on a web page, that happen based on user interactions like clicks, typing, scrolling, and more.

These effects can be things such as *pop-up ads*, animations, and much more (Eich and Dahl, n.d.). If you've ever used a form that instantly warns you about incorrect data without refreshing the page or a button that opens a dropdown menu, that's JavaScript at work.

Properties

What makes JavaScript unique from other programming languages is it is read and interpreted in the user's web browser during execution, as opposed to being compiled ahead of time and run by a separate application like *Java.*

This is why JavaScript is referred to as an **Interpreted** *or* **Just In Time (JIT) compiling language** (Doglio, 2020). This is often considered to be a good thing because it makes it easier for browsers to interpret and execute it.

JavaScript is generally run **synchronously**, which means the browser runs the code in the order in which it is written. It can also be run **asynchronously**, so if the code takes longer to execute, it will not block other parts of the document from being displayed.

This is important because it gives web developers the ability to make dynamic web pages that update automatically as the user interacts with the page.

Syntax

JavaScript Syntax or the unique set of rules the code must follow in order to be interpreted correctly by the browser. There are several key parts to JavaScript Syntax.

- First, it is case-sensitive, meaning changing the case of a letter can change the syntax of the code. For example, ***`FirstName`*** is not interpreted the same as ***`firstname`*** the browser would instead interpret these pieces of code as two different variables.

- Also, JavaScript uses a **unicode character set** which means developers have access to letters, numbers, and symbols from any language.

- Additionally, JavaScript statements are sometimes ended with a **semicolon** ; but this practice has fallen out of style in the programming community.

JavaScript syntax definitely goes much deeper than this, but these are some of the basics. In the next chapter, we will cover the more intricate aspects of JavaScript Syntax.

Chapter 3: JavaScript Syntax in Detail

Here are the additional key components of JavaScript syntax;**Variables, Data Types**, **Operators, Statements**, **Expressions**, **Functions**, **DOM Manipulation, Events, Conditional Statements**, **Loops,** and **Comments**. Understanding this is pivotal to being able to code JavaScript effectively.

Values

In JavaScript, **Values** can be thought of as pieces or chunks of information that are assigned to different numbers or pieces of text (Haverbeke, 2018).

In JavaScript syntax, two of the most common values are **Literals** and **Variables**. (W3School, n.d.)

- **Fixed values** - Literals
- **Changeable values** - Variables

Literals

Fixed values are also referred to as **Literals**, they are called "fixed values" because they are values that generally are not changed, once they are declared they remain as such. They can be **Numbers** written either with or without decimals like:

```
9.20
```

```
9001
```

Or **Strings** which are text, written within double or single quotes:

```
"John Doe"
```

```
'John Doe'
```

Both types of values can be used to store pieces of information. There are additional *Data Types* like **Boolean, Array, Objects,** and **symbols,** which are standalone entities or things with their own identity and properties. We will explore *Data Types* in more detail in its own section.

Each of these can be used to represent values as well, but Fixed values and strings are the most simplistic, and can help you establish a foundation for exploring more intricate values in the future.

Variables

As I mentioned**, Variables** are changeable values. A Variable can be declared using var, let, and const keywords, according to (Tutorialsteacher, .n.d.):

- var is a more archaic way to define a JavaScript variable. It has fallen out of use because it can cause confusion with other JavaScript keywords, and it has limited usage due to scoping issues.
- let removes the confusion and error of var. It is the new and recommended way of declaring variables in JavaScript.
- const is used to declare a constant variable that cannot be changed once assigned a value.

Variables can also be thought of as digital containers for holding Literal values. Revisiting the last example here are variables written with numbers (W3School, n.d.):

```
var x = 5;

let y = 6;

const z = x + y;
```

As you can see, the keywords `var`, `let`, and `const`, are used to designate variables. Additionally in the code snippet; **operators** are used to perform mathematical and logical operations between variables, as you can see the operators = and + were used. I will explain this concept and the code snippet in more detail in the next section.

Data Types

As I mentioned, in addition to Numbers, Literal Values and Variables can be represented by different *Data Types* like:

1. String:

A sequence of characters, used to represent text.

Example:

```
let greeting = "Hello, World!";
console.log(greeting); // Output: Hello, World!
```

---

2. Number:

Represents both integer and floating-point numbers, i.e. digits like 123

Example:

```
let age = 30;
let pi = 3.14;
console.log(age); // Output: 30
console.log(pi);  // Output: 3.14
```

---

3. Boolean:

Represents logical entities, having only two values: `true` or `false`.

Example:

```
let isDeveloper = true;
console.log(isDeveloper); // Output: true
```

---

4. Array:

An ordered list of values, or that can be referenced by name i.e. a collection of items (indexed elements).

Example:

```
let colors = ["red", "green", "blue"];
console.log(colors[1]); // Output: green
```

---

5. Object:

A collection of key-value pairs.

Example:

```
let person = {
  name: "Alice",
  age: 25,
  isStudent: false
};
console.log(person.name); // Output: Alice
```

---

6. Symbol:

A unique and immutable primitive value, often used as a key in object properties.

Example:

```
let sym = Symbol("uniqueKey");
let obj = {
  [sym]: "value"
};
console.log(obj[sym]); // Output: value
```

---

7. Undefined:

A variable that has been declared but not yet assigned a value.

Example:

```
let notAssigned;
console.log(notAssigned); // Output: undefined
```

---

8. Null:

Represents the intentional absence of any object value.

Example:

```
let emptyValue = null;
console.log(emptyValue); // Output: null
```

Operators

An **Operator** is a symbol that is used to perform a mathematical or logical operation between variables or values (W3School, n.d.).

Here's the code snippet example I referenced in the *Variable section*:

```
var x = 5;

var y = 6;

var z = x + y;
```

The symbol `=` is used to represent the **assignment operator** which is used to assign values to a specific symbol. In this case, it is used to show that the **letter X** is equal to 5 and **letter Y** is equal to 6.

Also the assignment operator is used in conjunction with the **addition operator** + to show that the **letter *Z*** is equal to the sum of letters **X** and **Y**.

There are other *arithmetic operators* such as:

Arithmetic operators

1. Subtraction (-):

Description: Subtracts the right-hand operand from the left-hand operand.

Example:

```
let result = 10 - 5; // result is 5
```

Explanation: Here, `10 - 5` equals `5`. The `-` operator simply subtracts the right-hand operand value of `5` from the left-hand operand value of `10`.

---

2. Multiplication Operator (*)

Description: The multiplication operator is used to multiply two numbers.

Example:

```
let a = 6;

let b = 4;

let result = a * b; // Multiplies 6 by 4

console.log(result); // Output: 24
```

Explanation: Here, `6 * 4` equals `24`. The `*` operator simply multiplies the two numbers on either side of it.

---

3. Division (/):

Description: Divides the left-hand operand by the right-hand operand.

Example:

```
let result = 10 / 2; // result is 5
```

Explanation: Here, `10 / 2` equals `5`. The `/` operator simply divides the left-hand operand `10` by the right-hand operand `2`.

---

4. Modulus (%):

Description: Returns the remainder of the division between two numbers.

Example:

```
let result = 10 % 3; // result is 1
```

Explanation: Here, `10 % 3` equals `1`. The `%` operator simply divides the left-hand operand `10` by the right-hand operand `3`. Because `10` divided by `3` gives a remainder of `1` the answer is `1`

Comparison Operators

Comparison operators help you perform logical comparisons in your JavaScript code, allowing you to control the flow of execution based on conditions. Here they are:

1. Equality (==)

Description: Compares two values for equality after converting them to a common type (type coercion).

Example:
```
console.log(5 == '5'); // true
```

Here, the string '5' is converted to a number before comparison.

---

2. Inequality (!=)

Description: Compares two values for inequality after type coercion.

Example:
```
console.log(5 != '6'); // true
```

The values are not equal, so it returns true.

---

3. Strict Equality (===)

Description: Compares two values for equality without type conversion (no coercion).

Example:
```
console.log(5 === '5'); // false
```

Here, the comparison fails because the types (number vs. string) are different.

---

4. Strict Inequality (!==)

Description: Compares two values for inequality without type conversion.

Example:
```
console.log(5 !== '5'); // true
```

The values are not equal due to different types, so it returns true.

---

5. Less Than (<)

Description: Checks if the left operand is less than the right operand.

Example:
```
console.log(5 < 10); // true
```

---

6. Greater Than (>)

Description: Checks if the left operand is greater than the right operand.

Example:
```
console.log(10 > 5); // true
```

---

7. Less Than or Equal To (<=)

Description: Checks if the left operand is less than or equal to the right operand.

Example:
```
console.log(5 <= 5); // true
```

---

8. Greater Than or Equal To (>=)

Description: Checks if the left operand is greater than or equal to the right operand.

Example:

```
console.log(10 >= 5); // true
```

Summary

- == and != : Perform type coercion.
- === and !== : No type coercion; strict checks.
- <, >, <=, >=: Compare numerical values.

These operators help you perform logical comparisons in your JavaScript code, allowing you to control the flow of execution based on conditions.

Logical Operators

Logical operators are used to combine or invert boolean values. The three main logical operators are:

Logical AND (&&):

Description: This operator returns `true` if both operands are true.

Example:

```
const a = true;

const b = false;

const result = a && b; // result is false
```

Explanation: Here, result is `false` because both `a` and `b` must be true for the result to be `true`.

Logical OR (`||`):

Description: This operator returns `true` if at least one of the operands is true.

Example:

```
const a = true;

const b = false;

const result = a || b; // result is true
```

Explanation: In this case, result is `true` because `a` is true, so the overall expression evaluates to true.

Logical NOT (`!`):

Description: This operator inverts the boolean value of its operand.

Example:

```
const a = true;

const result = !a; // result is false
```

Explanation: Here, result is `false` because the NOT operator flips `true` to `false`.

Combining Logical Operators

You can also combine these operators to create more complex conditions:

```
const x = 5;

const y = 10;
```

```
const isGreater = (x > 3) && (y < 15); // isGreater is true

const isEither = (x < 3) || (y > 15); // isEither is false

const notTrue = !(x === 5); // notTrue is false
```

Explanation: In this example:

`isGreater is true` because both conditions are true.

`isEither is false` because neither condition is true.

`notTrue is false` because the expression `x === 5` is true, and the NOT operator inverts it.

These logical operators are fundamental in controlling the flow of your code, especially in conditional statements.

typeof Operator

The `typeof` operator in JavaScript is used to determine the type of a variable or an expression. It returns a string indicating the type. Here are some examples along with explanations:

Example 1: Basic Types

```
console.log(typeof "Hello, World!"); // "string"

console.log(typeof 42);              // "number"

console.log(typeof true);             // "boolean"

console.log(typeof undefined);        // "undefined"

console.log(typeof null);             // "object" (this is a
known quirk in JavaScript)
```

Explanation:

- `typeof "Hello, World!"` returns `"string"` because it's a string value.
- `typeof 42` returns `"number"` since 42 is a numeric value.
- `typeof true` returns `"boolean"` because it's a boolean value.
- `typeof undefined` returns `"undefined"` when a variable has been declared but not assigned a value.
- `typeof null` returns `"object"` due to a historical bug in JavaScript.

Example 2: Complex Types

```
console.log(typeof { name: "Alice", age: 30 }); // "object"

console.log(typeof [1, 2, 3]);                     //
"object" (arrays are also objects)

console.log(typeof function() {});                  // "function"

console.log(typeof new Date());                     // "object"
```

Explanation:

- `typeof { name: "Alice", age: 30 }` returns `"object"` because it's an object literal.
- `typeof [1, 2, 3]` returns `"object"` because arrays are technically objects in JavaScript.
- `typeof function() {}` returns `"function"` since functions are first-class objects.
- `typeof new Date()` returns `"object"` because a Date is also an object.

Example 3: Checking for Specific Types

```
let variable = "Hello";
```

```
if (typeof variable === "string") {

    console.log("It's a string!");

} else {

    console.log("It's not a string.");

}
```

Explanation: In this example, we check if `variable` is of type `"string"` using the `typeof` operator. If it is, we log "It's a string!". In this case the variable is `"Hello";` which is a string because it's letters so the console should log `It's a string!`

Summary

The `typeof` operator is useful for type checking and debugging, allowing developers to understand the data types they are working with in their code.

Bitwise XOR Operator

The ^ operator is a bitwise XOR (exclusive OR) operator. It compares two numbers on a bit level (binary) and returns 1 when the bits are different and 0 when they are the same.

Example:

```
let num1 = 5;   // Binary: 101

let num2 = 3;   // Binary: 011

let result = num1 ^ num2; // XOR: 110 (6 in decimal)

console.log(result); // Output: 6
```

Explanation:

- 5 in binary is `101`

- `3` in binary is `011`
- XOR compares the bits:
  - 1 ^ 0 = 1
  - 0 ^ 1 = 1
  - 1 ^ 0 = 0
- So the result is `110` (which is 6 in decimal).

Bitwise XOR can be useful in programming for various tasks, like:

- Finding differences between numbers.
- Swapping values without a temporary variable.
- Creating checksums for data verification.

As you can see, there is an operator to represent virtually every mathematical or logical operation.

Statements

Statements are lines of code that instruct the browser to perform a specific task or function. They are essentially a sequence of operators, values and expressions that are grouped together meant to be interpreted in a specific order or fashion (W3School, n.d.).

Here's an example of a statement (W3School, n.d.):

```
let x, y, z;

x = 7;

y = 3;

z = x + y;
```

As you can see the statement is used to instruct the browser on how to solve `Z = X + Y`, which based on the instruction should be `10`.

Expressions

An expression is an example of a *statement*, it is a combination of values, variables, and operators.

Essentially it is a sequence of calculations that lead to a unique value, like a number sentence such as; `5 + 3` = the value of `8` or `2*3` = the value of `6` (Brainstation, 2022) .

Examples of expressions include arithmetic operations (you may recall these from the ***operators section***) such as + addition, - subtraction, * multiplication, and / division, as well as && logical and == comparison operations.

As you can see from the examples, the symbols used in each expression are the same as the JavaScript operators mentioned earlier.

Functions

Functions are a code snippet that includes "procedures" or a set of statements and expressions that are grouped together for a specific purpose or to perform a task. Essentially they are meant to be used over and over again as opposed to creating a new function for every use (Brainstation, 2022).

Here's an example (W3Schools, n.d.):

```
function toCelsius(fahrenheit) {
  return (5/9) * (fahrenheit-32);
}
document.getElementById("demo").innerHTML = toCelsius(77);
```

The function includes several key parts:

```
function toCelsius(fahrenheit)
```

This statement identifies the function or procedure to be completed, in this case, the procedure is to convert Fahrenheit to Celsius.

Next part of the code snippet:

```
{  return (5/9) * (fahrenheit-32);}
```

This statement indicates the sequence of expressions to be completed in order to `return` the answer to the question.

Essentially the statement is saying to convert a Fahrenheit measurement to Celsius, the following steps must first be completed; Divide `5/9`, and take the inputted Fahrenheit measurement minus `- 32`. Then take the result of these two expressions and multiply * them. As you can see the order in which these operations are performed is important in order to return the correct answer.

Then the last statement:

```
document.getElementById("demo").innerHTML = toCelsius(77);
```

Is instructing the computer to show the answer to the function on the user's screen via HTML more specifically as an HTML tag with the `id "demo"` (We will explore *DOM (Dynamic Object Model)* manipulation) in the next section.

The last part of the statement `toCelsius(77);` between the parentheses `()` is where the programmer would input the Fahrenheit number they wish to be converted.

In this case, the Fahrenheit number inputted was 77F. So the result should be 25C.

Again as you can see functions are great because they allow you to write reusable pieces of code. Instead of repeating yourself, you define a function and use it multiple times throughout your program.

DOM (Document Object Model) Manipulation

The **Document Object Model (DOM)** represents the structure of a webpage as a tree of objects. Each element on the page is part of this tree. JavaScript allows you to access and manipulate the DOM, which enables dynamic updates to the HTML content. You can use the graphic I included below from wikipedia to help you with making sense of the DOM.

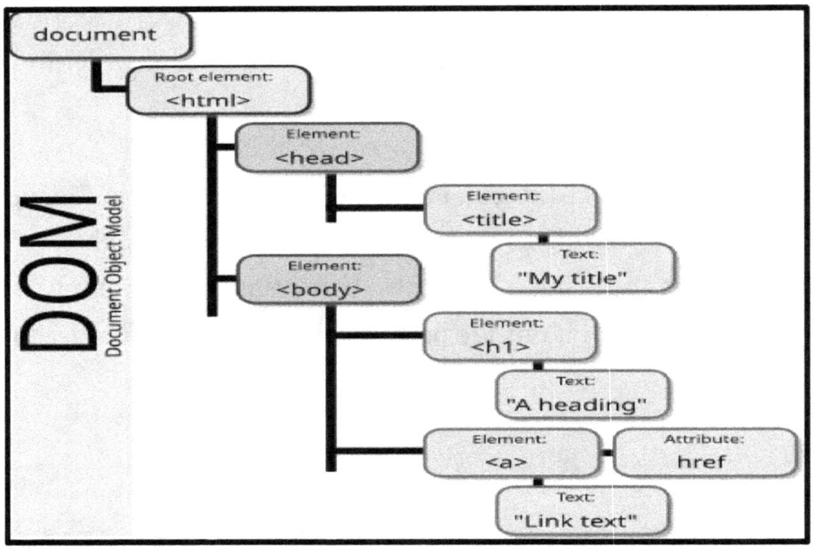

Cited From: https://en.wikipedia.org/wiki/Document_Object_Model

As you can recall from the *functions section* with the Fahrenheit to Celsius function, we used DOM manipulation to show the answer to the function on the user's screen via HTML more specifically as an HTML tag with the `id "demo"`

Here are some more additional things you can do with DOM manipulation. For example, you can:

- Change the content of an element.
- Modify the styles dynamically.
- Add or remove elements from the page.

Let’s look at another example of DOM manipulation in action:

```
document.getElementById("heading").innerHTML = "New Heading Text";
```

This line of JavaScript will change the content of an HTML element with the ID `heading` to `"New Heading Text"`. As you can see DOM manipulation is an excellent way to bring static webpages to life.

Events

An **Event** is a signal or alert that is triggered when users interact with an HTML element on a webpage (W3School, n.d.).

Essentially events are actions or occurrences that happen in the browser, like clicking a button, hovering over a link, or submitting a form. JavaScript allows you to "listen" for these events and respond to them.

Here's an example of an HTML code snippet that just uses the event `onlick` which tells the browser to trigger an event when a button `<button>` is clicked on:

```
<button onclick="displayDate()">The time is?</button>
```

This particular event is instructing the browser to display a date, when the `button` is clicked on (W3School, n.d.).

JavaScript can also listen for other events, such as `mouseover`, `keypress`, and `load`. As you can see, Events are a great way to build interactive web pages.

Conditional Statements

Conditional statements determine whether or not pieces of code can run, or if it is true or false. (W3Schools, n.d.). Essentially, you use them to execute code only if certain conditions are met.

There are three main types of conditional statements:

`if` statements: where if a condition is <u>true</u> it is used to specify execution for a block of code.

`else` statements: where if the same condition is <u>false</u> it specifies the execution for a block of code.

`else if` statements: this specifies a new test if the first condition is false.

Here's a code snippet example:

```
let num = 7;
```

```
if (num > 10) {
  console.log("The number is greater than 10.");
} else if (num > 5) {
  console.log("The number is greater than 5 but less than or equal
to 10.");
} else {
  console.log("The number is less than or equal to 5.");
}
```

The `let num = 7` indicates that the variable `num` will be assigned a value of `7`.

The `if` statement; `if (num > 10)` checks whether the value of the `num` variable is greater than `10`. If the statement is `true` then the text: `("The number is greater than 10.")` will be displayed on the user's console.

Since `num` is actually `7`, this condition is `false`, so the next statement `else if (num > 5)` will be executed instead.

If the statement is `true` for this piece of code, then the text: `("The number is greater than 5 but less than or equal to 10.")` will be displayed on the user's console.

But if the answer is `false`, then `else` statement is executed; if the value of `num` is less than `5`, then the console will instead log: `("The number is less than or equal to 5.")`

As you can see, Conditional statements are a significant part of JavaScript programming and are a great way to make the code more dynamic and responsive to user input or other changing conditions.

Loops

In JavaScript, loops are used to repeatedly execute a block of code as long as a specified condition is true. This allows you to automate repetitive tasks, iterate over data structures like arrays, or perform actions a set number of times. There are several types of loops in JavaScript:

1. `for` Loop

The `for` loop is commonly used when you know in advance how many times you want to iterate.

```
for (let i = 0; i < 5; i++) {

  console.log(i); // Output: 0, 1, 2, 3, 4

}
```

- **Initialization**: `let i = 0;` — This runs once at the start of the loop.
- **Condition**: `i < 5;` — The loop continues as long as this condition is true.
- **Increment/Update**: `i++` — This runs after each iteration.

---

2. `while` Loop

The `while` loop repeats as long as a specified condition is true.

```
let i = 0;

while (i < 5) {

  console.log(i);

  i++;

}
```

---

3. `do...while` Loop

The `do...while` loop is similar to the `while` loop, but it ensures that the loop runs at least once, even if the condition is initially false.

```
let i = 0;

do {

  console.log(i);

  i++;
```

```
} while (i < 5);
```

---

4. `for...of` Loop

This loop iterates over iterable objects like arrays, strings, or sets.

```
let array = [10, 20, 30];
for (let value of array) {
  console.log(value); // Output: 10, 20, 30
}
```

---

5. `for...in` Loop

This loop iterates over the keys of an object or an array's indices.

```
let obj = { a: 1, b: 2, c: 3 };
for (let key in obj) {
  console.log(key); // Output: a, b, c
}
```

Key Points:

- `for` is for a defined number of iterations.
- `while` is for conditional looping until the condition is false.
- `for...of` iterates over values of an iterable.
- `for...in` iterates over keys (properties or indices).

These looping mechanisms help to perform repetitive tasks efficiently in JavaScript.

Comments

To inform others about the instructions of the JavaScript code, developers are able to write **Comments**.

The comments also give the observer info on the **semantics** or the meaning of the code. (W3Schools, n.d.)
To indicate a single line comment, a user inputs double slashes //

Also any code that is between the slashes; / and / is treated as a comment also.

Lastly, according to W3Schools, a comment can also be used to stop a line of code from being executed, for testing purposes. (W3Schools, n.d.)

Here's an example of comments in action:

Code Snippet A: `let x = 5;    // I will be executed`

Code Snippet B: `// x = 6;    I will NOT be executed`

As you can see from the example, **Code Snippet A** will be executed, because the expression `let x = 5;` is included before the double slashes //. While **Code Snippet B** will not be executed because the expression `x = 6;` is not included before the double slashes.

Overall, JavaScript comments are pretty straight forward, and they are good to use when you need to provide information about what the code is being used for. Also if you want to stop a line of code from being executed so you can test the code.

In the next section we are going to explore the different ways in which JavaScript can be added to an HTML document. This will help you will be able to implement JavaScript yourself.

Chapter 4: How JavaScript is Added to HTML

JavaScript can be implemented on web pages in one of three ways:

1. Inline
2. External
3. Internally

Again, each has its own pros and cons.

Internal JavaScript

If JavaScript is written directly in an HTML document, a <script> tag in the <head> section of the document with the `language` and `type` attributes added indicates the code has been added.

Here's an example of a series of functions (Tutorialspoint, n.d.):

```
<head>
     <script language = "javascript" type = "text/javascript">
(function (w, d, s, l, i) {
        w[l] = w[l] || [];
        w[l].push({ "gtm.start": new Date().getTime(), event:
"gtm.js" });
        var f = d.getElementsByTagName(s)[0],
          j = d.createElement(s),
          dl = l != "dataLayer" ? "&l=" + l : "";
        j.async = true;
        j.src = "https://www.googletagmanager.com/gtm.js?id=" +
i + dl;
        f.parentNode.insertBefore(j, f);
      })(window, document, "script", "dataLayer", "GTM-
KVL636G");

     </script>
</head>
```

As you can see the code snippet is *nested* inside the `<head>` tags and the *`language`* and `type` attributes were added to the `<script>` tag to indicate that a JavaScript code snippet is being added.

The "code" nested in the `<script>` tag is an example of a *tracking pixel* which is a piece of JavaScript code used to track a webpage user's actions on the page.

Pros and Cons

Pros:

- Generally takes up less space

Cons:

- If in the `<head>` section it can slow down the webpage (render-blocking)
- May be harder to maintain and reuse code

External JavaScript

The code can also be loaded through an *external* file with the `.js` extension and then loading it within the page with again a `<script>` tag, and an [`src`] attribute added to the script tag, here's an example:

```
<body>
    <script src="name of file.js"></script>
</body>
```

The code does not necessarily need to be nested in the `<head>` tag. In this case, the code is being loaded from the `<body>` section of the HTML document.

Here are some pros and cons of external JavaScript, according to K.V. (2021):

Pros and Cons

Pros:

- Easy to reuse code.
- Easier to read
- Easier to compress and minify

Cons:

- The browser has to make an extra HTTP request to get the `.js` code.
- Code can be downloaded using the URL of the `.js` file. This can help coders to steal your code easily.
- If two `.js` files are dependent on one another, then a failure in one file may affect the execution of the other dependent file.
- A small change to a common `.js` file may cause unexpected results in some of the HTML files.

Inline JavaScript

Lastly, you can add the JavaScript code *inline* or directly inside an HTML tag, and then add **attributes** to the tag that trigger an action when interacted with such as:

- `onclick` (when the object is clicked on by the user)
- `onmouseover` (when the user moves their mouse)
- `onkeypress` (when the user presses a specific key on their keyboard)
- `onload` (when the user loads the webpage), etc.

These are also considered to be examples of **JavaScript Events** (recall the *Events section*)

Here's an example:

```
<button onclick="alert('Hello World!')">Click Me</button>
```

As you can see the attribute `onclick` was added with the action to show a display box with the text "Hello world" when the button is clicked on (Tutorial Republic n.d.).

Here are the Pros and Cons for this method:

Pros and Cons

Pros:

- Generally takes up less space

Cons:

- Harder to maintain code

- Difficult to reuse code for other projects
- Unable to be *cached* or saved for future use by Web Browsers

Last Words About JavaScript

JavaScript is an essential tool for every web developer. It allows you to go beyond static content and create engaging, interactive websites that respond to user input.

Whether it's adding a simple button click event or building an entire web application, JavaScript is the key to unlocking dynamic functionality on the web.

Chapter 5: Practice Activities

Now that you've learned the basics of JavaScript, it's time to test your understanding with some hands-on practice. Practice is essential for mastering web development, and the more you experiment with JavaScript, the more you'll solidify the concepts you've learned.

In this chapter, we will present a series of exercises that focus on key JavaScript concepts like manipulating the DOM, handling events, working with variables, and controlling the flow of a program.

These exercises are designed to help you build interactive web pages with basic JavaScript functionality. By completing them, you'll gain confidence in applying your JavaScript knowledge to actual projects.

---

1. Displaying Text with JavaScript

Question: Create a simple webpage and use JavaScript to display text dynamically:

- A heading that says "Hello, JavaScript!" should appear when the page loads.
- Add a button that, when clicked, changes the heading to say "You clicked the button!"

Hint: Use `document.getElementById()` to select the heading and `addEventListener()` to trigger a function when the button is clicked.

---

2. Simple Math Operations

Question: Write a JavaScript program that performs basic math operations:

- Create two variables: one with the value 10 and another with the value 5.
- Display the result of adding, subtracting, multiplying, and dividing these numbers in the browser.

Hint: Use JavaScript arithmetic operators (+, -, *, /) and `console.log()` or `document.write()` to display the results.

---

3. Changing Element Style with JavaScript

Question: Create a webpage that allows users to change the style of an element:

- Add a paragraph of text that says, "Change my color!" and a button.
- When the button is clicked, change the text color to red.

Hint: Use `document.querySelector()` to select the paragraph and `style.color` to change its color.

---

4. Handling User Input

Question: Create a simple form and use JavaScript to handle the user input:

- Add a text input field and a button.
- When the user types something and clicks the button, display the typed text below the form.

Hint: Use `document.getElementById()` to get the value of the input field, and `innerHTML` to display the text on the page.

---

5. Building a Simple Counter

Question: Create a webpage with a simple counter:

- Add a button that says "Click Me!" and a paragraph that starts with "Clicks: 0".
- Each time the button is clicked, increment the counter and update the paragraph to show the new count.

Hint: Use a JavaScript variable to store the count, and update the text using `innerHTML` or `textContent`.

---

6. Basic Event Handling

Question: Set up event handlers to respond to user actions:

- Create a webpage with a button that says "Hover over me!".
- When the user hovers over the button, change its background color to green.
- When the mouse leaves the button, change the background color back to its original color.

Hint: Use `addEventListener()` for `mouseover` and `mouseout` events.

---

7. Simple To-Do List

Question: Build a basic to-do list using JavaScript:

- Add an input field and a button to allow the user to type in a task.
- When the user clicks the button, the task should be added as a list item below the input field.

Hint: Use `createElement()` to create new list items and `appendChild()` to add them to the page.

---

8. Creating a Random Number Generator

Question: Write a JavaScript program that generates random numbers:

- Add a button that says "Generate Random Number."
- When the button is clicked, display a random number between 1 and 100 on the page.

Hint: Use `Math.random()` and `Math.floor()` to generate the random number.

---

9. Basic Conditional Statements

Question: Create a webpage that responds to user input with a conditional statement:

- Add a text input field where the user can type their age.
- When the user clicks a button, display a message saying "You are old enough to drive!" if the age is 16 or older. Otherwise, display "You are not old enough to drive."

Hint: Use an `if-else` statement to compare the user's input.

---

10. Simple Loops

Question: Write a JavaScript program that uses a loop:

- Create a button that, when clicked, displays the numbers from 1 to 5 on the page.

Hint: Use a `for` loop to iterate through the numbers and `innerHTML` to display them on the page.

Conclusion

These 10 practice activities are designed to cover a range of essential JavaScript skills, from basic DOM manipulation and event handling to user input and simple conditional logic. By working through these exercises, you will reinforce what you have learned and start applying JavaScript to real-world scenarios.

As you complete each task, review the output in your browser to ensure that the JavaScript behaves as expected. Remember: mastering JavaScript takes practice. The more you work through exercises like these, the more comfortable you'll become with writing interactive code, setting the foundation for more advanced topics like animations, AJAX, and JavaScript frameworks.

Chapter 6: Last Thoughts

As we come to the conclusion of this journey, it's important to step back and reflect on what you've learned about the essential components of web development—JavaScript.

JavaScript is the programming language that brings websites to life. While HTML provides the structure and CSS offers the design, JavaScript enables dynamic interactivity, transforming static web pages into engaging, responsive experiences. It powers everything from form validation, interactive elements, and animations to complex web applications and real-time data updates.

By learning JavaScript, you've acquired the skills to add interactivity and functionality to web content. You've explored different JavaScript features, from basic syntax and control structures to working with the DOM (Document Object Model) and handling events. You've learned how to make websites dynamic, responding to user input, and creating more personalized, engaging experiences. These are essential tools that allow you to build interactive, responsive websites.

Learning JavaScript is like learning how to think programmatically—it gives you the power to automate tasks, solve complex problems, and enhance the overall user experience. But like any skill, mastery comes with continuous practice and exploration. There's always something new to learn—whether it's refining your understanding of asynchronous programming, exploring modern JavaScript frameworks like React or Vue, or experimenting with new features introduced in the latest versions of ECMAScript.

The best way to improve your JavaScript skills is by applying them to real-world projects. Start with smaller projects like interactive forms, simple games, or dynamic landing pages, where you can experiment with different programming techniques. Over time, you can tackle more complex challenges like single-page applications (SPAs) or integrating APIs to fetch real-time data, using advanced techniques such as promises, async/await, and modular JavaScript.

Each project will help you grow as a developer, whether it's discovering new ways to optimize your code or finding more efficient methods to enhance performance. The more you build, the deeper your understanding of how JavaScript shapes the user experience will become.

Remember, web development isn't just about coding—it's also about creativity, problem-solving, and an ongoing commitment to learning. Keep experimenting, keep refining your code, and most importantly, enjoy the creative process.

Thank you for joining me on this journey. The web is a vast space with endless opportunities for creativity and innovation. Now, it's your turn to take what you've learned and build something amazing!

About the Author

Roggie (Raj) Clark, is a 9 year SEO professional and owner of the SEO agency; *Bounce Rank.* Prior to joining the SEO industry, Raj was a web developer and school teacher. It was through creating his own websites, and wanting a career change from teaching, that Raj stumbled across the world of SEO.

Since joining the field nearly a decade ago, Raj has worked on a wide range of campaigns, from eCommerce, to B2B, to Healthcare, for enterprise companies and marketing agencies in the United States.

He is regarded as an expert, and guru by his colleagues, and the SEO industry. Raj currently lives in Maryland with his sister and niece.

www.ingramcontent.com/pod-product-compliance
Lightning Source LLC
LaVergne TN
LVHW080528210926
848481LV00022B/3645